MW00572348

I AM A
FURIOUS
WISH

ANTHOLOGY OF
LOWCOUNTRY POETS
VOLUME ONE
2022

FREE VERSE PRESS
A FREE VERSE, LLC EXPERIENCE

Copyright © 2022 Free Verse, LLC

All rights reserved. No part of this publication may be reproduced, distributed, or transmitted in any form or by any means, including photocopying, recording, or other electronic or mechanical methods, without the prior written permission of the publisher, except in the case of brief quotations embodied in critical reviews and certain other noncommercial uses permitted by copyright law.

For permission requests, write to the publisher, addressed "Attention: Permissions Coordinator," at the website below.

ISBN: 978-1-7374696-6-7

Library of Congress Control Number: 2022941636

Book design by Marcus Amaker

Printed in the United States of America.

First printing edition 2022

Published by Free Verse Press
Free Verse, LLC
Charleston, South Carolina

freeversepress.com

TABLE OF CONTENTS

Amy Drennan

Ashton Fludd

Austin Hehir

Charles Watts

Christian Morant

Cory Stegelin

Emily Wingfield

Evangeline Sanders

Frances J. Pearce

Gracie Bell

Hailey Williams

Harold Oberman

Jean Catherine Hubbard

John Luke Byrne

John Schumacher

Kaylin Moss

Latanya Mueller

Linda Joy Walder

Lucinda Rowekamp

Maci Petrolle

Marilyn Cox

Natasha Akery

Randy Milledge

Roger Mindwater

Samajema Davis

Shelia L. Anderson

Yvette R. Murray

Zania Cummings

Double-Dog Dare

I dare you to love me
when I won't die,
when I outrun trains,
take corners on two wheels,
am one wheel short
of four on the floor.
I dare you.

I take medicine
for the medicine,
don't believe in medicine.
Sick as the secrets,
believe in secrets.

I dare you to love me
when I suck in my stomach,
when I play thin,
walk the thin line,
thicken in your hands.
Love me when I grow round
under your fingers.

I dare you to see me
when I make myself invisible,
when eyes are not enough,
when eye contact hurts,
is held like hot iron,
scars,
and makes us stronger.

I dare you wet feet
on marble tile.

The trill of it.
The ice-cold chase
without slipping.
I dare you
to chase me.

I dare you naked,
unhiding,
unmasked though the world
may be ending.
I dare you
undressed.

I dare you the eye
of a tiny tornado.
The coming to.
The How did I get here?
of this.

I dare you fighting,
apologizing,
choosing me
again, and again.
I dare you hanging on when it hurts,
when you wish to let go.

I dare you four major pathways.
The pleasure. The reward.
I wish you the feel-good.
I wish you desire, sensation.
I wish you dopamine.

I dare you a chain-link
of fears voiced.
Things to be cut through.

Things you don't speak of.
I wish you a bolt-cutter-heart.
I wish you the right tool
at the right time.

I dare you the basics.
Warm bed,
soft pillow.
Someone to untangle the knots
with you.
Someone who sees
you are tangled.
Someone unafraid.

I dare you courage.
I dare you superhero-strength.

I dare you,
don't lose
your soft side.

I dare you to decide
what you're willing to kill.
What makes space for what?
Where are these boundaries
you speak of?

I dare you step over.
Cross the line.
Line up,
though you be one
and I make two.

I double-dog dare you.
Be worth the risk.

— *Amy Drennan*

I blame you, this counting.

Months. Days. Hours.

What good is it
if only I care?
What heartbreak
if we both do?

Mountains don't move
when we're watching.
So many mountains
never moved.

I kiss you as I'd like
to be remembered.
I kiss you the way
I'll remember us.

I sing from where
I've always sung.
From the base of my spine.
Tips of my toes.
Back of my throat.
Electric.

I make music of myself.
Wish to be mix-taped,
road-tripped,
ripped at the top of a lung,
your lung.

My small hands
protect you from me,

us from us.
My small hands
fit perfectly.

My sidesaddle is a safe space,
imagination greedy,
thick fingered,
hungry all the time.

I pull weeds,
my hair out,
the single thread
that unravels it all.

I pull back,
myself together,
apologies stuffed in my pockets.
I pull a fast one.

You,
lover of mountain air,
hard lefts,
first snows.
I would freeze you in place
if you'd stand still.

I would count you
a winter for the ages.
A never-warm-without-me
season.

I'd count the fires you've set.

I count myself
as almost costing you
the forest.

— *Amy Drennan*

Compeer

Can pluck nine croutons
out of a bowl
without swallowing
a single lettuce leaf.

Can suck Parmesan threads
through the eye of a salad's needle,
never let on
that he's guilty.

Reminds me
a good tummy rub
is all that's needed.

Flip yourself over.
Find a person worth trusting.
Expose your belly,
practice breathing.

He curls himself in under breast.
Tiny deer feet
cradled in my hand.

Little snake plant,
he thrives on neglect.
Is happiest AFTER left alone.
Is happiest
when I come back.

Small recognizes small,
loves it back into itself.
Big eyes,

soft, wet snout.

Can hear a branch break
miles away.
Can run nearly as fast
as a squirrel.
Appalled each time
he can't catch it.

Can smell yes and no.
No,
is a low growl.
Yes,
a top-of-the-foot-lick,
sunshine trust.

When I deign
to set myself on fire,
here he comes,
tiny extinguisher.
Licks me like burning
is a bad idea.
Licks to remind me,
I promised.

This itty-bitty therapist
is ever so gentle.
Allows me my bad days.
Allows me
me.

I wish to be more dog-like.
My midriff
an invitation.
My fear a thing

I can shake off.

Canine love
waltzes into itself,
raises a leg,
marks its territory.
Canine love
has no shame.

Our love is emotional support.
Our love flies free
if it fits under the seat.

A friend spoke of death
as my dog
kissed his ankle.

Ankle kisses mean
I'm listening.
When no one else listens,
he does.

— *Amy Drennan*

Belief in Eventual Spring

You,
magnificent disaster,
did you ever really love me?
Did we love?

Were you tethered
through the belly,
are we tethered?

We did not know
each other's names.
Your mother and I,
did not know
each other's names.

Water will rise to meet us,
water did rise.
Swimming boy,
swam fast,
paddled hard,
practiced.
The middle of the road
did rise to meet you.

We made lists of things
we wouldn't get done today.
Checked off all we didn't do,
failed to do a thing but us.

We took what happened to us,
used it to heal others,
this is how we helped,

how we mattered,
how we didn't end when we ended.

Jealousy and pride
are BLTs at midnight...
not made for me.
Jealousy and pride are consort,
a daughter I've named,
will never have.

Tennyson Grace,
did you know your papa
was a closeted wordsmith,
a man who chased birds,
a man who chased demons
out of our house?

Did you know your papa
had a voice like mine,
a throat that choked on everything,
hands that held it all together?

Your daddy made casserole,
held space,
wished on stars for you.
Your daddy wished on stars.
You would have been a star.

Forgive this love,
the unborn,
the star-crossedness of it all.

Forgive the quiet,
the too many words.
It was my fault and not.

We rarely rained at the same time
but we did rain.
From here to wherever
has always been wet,
has always been a sky
about to break open.
Before we knew rain.
Before we knew sky.

Faith is blue,
forgiving the unforgivable,
a bad signal.
Faith plants trees
out of season.

Spring is a voluntary heartbreak.
A risk.
A feather
that's lost its wing.

— *Amy Drennan*

Montage

A montage of moments allow glimpses
Into a treasure trove of melancholia.
Phobias of my adolescence courted my insecurities,
At the age of eleven it was ingrained in my psyche.
Be leery of pretenders so called friends with hidden
agendas.
Keeping my distance is where I've been.

— *Ashton Flood*

Breathing

I've been conditioned to avoid confrontation.
Walking away is as easy as breathing.

— *Ashton Flood*

Humbled

Humbled by the fight or flight response
I dwell in fear,
Fear of questions that need to be answered.
Going through the motions
I won't dare to challenge my beliefs.
I grow weary, however this is where I made my home.

— *Ashton Flood*

See Me

You brought me to my knees.
Like mere mortals in the king's presence
I praised you, wanting you to acknowledge my
 existence,
Hoping you'd see me as a human being.

— Ashton Flood

Fool

Make a fool out of me,
You don't care about my feelings.
Pick on me when I'm feeling low,
Apologize and I'll let it go.
I'll do anything, anything to fit in.

— Ashton Flood

permission

I exchanged my life the other day.
Time in. Money out. The banal banter of bureaucratic
sacraments.
You have permission.

Ventricles splintered from consumed termites,
buried deep in the framework, left my chest heavy with
the weight of lost time.
I exchanged my life the other day.

I've got a bad case of *the horrors*
still scored from past transactions I can't remember and
future debts forever unpaid.
You have permission.

Obligated in forfeiture, it cost merely to be.
Monetizing moments of manufactured engrossment,
lives lay broken and bare in front of us.
I exchanged my life the other day.

Vapid decay caked on the cherry blossoms' roots.
I missed the pure production, exchanging life for subtle
emotions without cause in the world.
You have permission.

Even amongst the terror,
especially amongst the terror. Because from joy, comes
hope.
I exchanged my life the other day.

But this time for joy.
I gave myself permission.

— *Austin Hehir*

beautiful days

I've grown to resent beautiful days in December.
Dripping by like a weeping anesthetic
slowly amongst our heat.

Sun beats on the bruised earth, weathering
the hectic burns of *consumption*.
Night sweats shaking the bones.

I crave the days of snow soaked flurries
and mild manner fevers, imprinted in
genetic code of lifetimes ago.

Lost are long drives across our country's sides.
Coughing foliage left to rot, looking up at stars.
Eyes soaked in the insatiable and insensible
abscess.

Flared and running red,
hiding behind a withered
and cryptic cough.

Scents of summer bonfires made from winter's
dried pine maligned by the malady
to the smells of congested brine.

Buds burnt, gagging on the decrepit taste.
Engrossed by our narcotic and carbonic
lust for growth.

Glorious waves of coastal shores no longer
fill me with swelling joy.
That wasting away, our bodily erosion.
Never to rise to the rise.
Left to our slowly prescribed demise
where we have beautiful days in December.

— *Austin Hehir*

hero

In the shadow of the fentanyl drip, an elderly woman feels the details of her life carving out spaces in her head. A mess of a man comes to her bedside, not ready. The doctors huddle around the bed as the machine's buzzes and ticks tremble to a final crescendo. She says hello to him, the mess of a man. He is but a witness now, to her life and for what it was worth.

Saint Vitus's dance
comes for us all in time.
And then I stumbled.

— Austin Hehir

the sun is more than a star

It was dawn and dusk: a *civil twilight*
casting aside the day as the snake sheds its skin.
I love the night like an alcoholic,
the sun's whispers chatter to the skull.

I trace the notches of my spine,
finding the supple viscera of the pain.
Where the guts and marrow of life linger.
It was dawn and dusk: *a civil twilight*

Fuck the stars, they're full of hot air.
Wrinkles in the smile of a face
forced to that flaccid facade,
casting aside the day as the snake sheds its skin.

Psych ward sycophants seizing
frayed strings like a bird builds its nest.
Searching for those little slivers of death that evade.
I love the night like an alcoholic.

Nothing left but the labors of pain and static
left falling through our broken planks of reason.
And then the night gives way to a new day.
The sun's whispers chatter to the skull.

— *Austin Hehir*

letters

I hold my secrets to the light, hoping that they'd burn.
Engraved in my flesh, that carcinomic return.
I can only breathe in the places between
what I have lost and what I have yet to learn.

Remember me with an aggregate sheen
and not my *debrided* state as foreseen.
Take some gum. It helps with the smell.
Even our palettes turn gagged green.

Owls of Minerva fly at night's bell
and no child should tell their parents farewell.
I hope I find those iambic feet,
Passing by in a four-four swell.

Take in these moments, made from heat.
The strange time before my final feat.
Where everything still can be redeemed.
Where everything still - can be redeemed.

— *Austin Hehir*

A Seemingly Happy Fellow

A seemingly happy fellow
Smiling under a banyan tree
Instructed me to tape a natural pearl
Under my armpit or I would die
In three days. I asked him why.

Because, he said, I had sought him out
Because, he said, he had planted the thought
Because, he said, once planted it must grow
Because, he said, I say so

You of course, he said, have free will
You of course, he sighed, will think me
A daft old fraud wasting his life
Under a banyan tree

I will pray for you at the funeral
I will ask that you be spared
Ten thousand rebirths into sorrow and regret
Or you could just tape on the damned pearl
And see what happens next

— *Charles Watts*

If This Were the Marshlands

If this were the marshlands
And there were no trees
Or hills or highrises
To muddle the horizon
The harvest moon
Would already have risen

But here in the mountains
Where the wind whips
The clouds across
The canvas of the sky
Heaven Hill
Blocks the moonrise

It has been a summer
Of clouds and rain
A summer of seldom
Stars, of unseen
Meteor showers, of
No northern lights

It has been good
For the mushrooms
For the lichen
For the black cohosh
For the hostas
And the deer

But we have waited
Past the equinox to
Birth this envious moon
Later than the Almanac
Says it should appear
But in its own good time

— *Charles Watts*

You Ask If I Am Well

I am well
I am at peace
I am cold as vaccine in dry ice

I am facing life
I turn my back on hate
I feel sometimes alone

I am slow to judge
I am quick to forgive
I lie each time I speak

You are kind to ask
You are the first
To ask

I am sorry
You had to listen
To what is left of me

— *Charles Watts*

Poetry Night at the Library

no one rises from the hush
throws a fist in the air
shatters the silence with cries of

Oh Yes Brother/Oh Yes Sister

that is it, that is the truth
that is the feeling I have
always wanted to be

that is the place I have
only been in dreams of worlds
broken and resurrected, torn asunder

and reborn

they sit and wait
for the end of the reading
hands steaming in frozen laps

wait for the words to
clatter and crumple
out of the vapor

and finally stop

and only then polite applause
oh do not let me remember
the words or the silence

but only the blood
that swelled my face
the light that shined
through your eyes into mine

— *Charles Watts*

The Current Above

"Grieve not; though the journey of life be bitter, and the end unseen, there is no road which does not lead to an end."
Hafez

Day off or off-day
Plans made or canceled
Dreams fulfilled or lying
In tatters, buried in the humus
On some forest floor
Burrowing deep
Into the surface of things
We sometimes find life
The only thing we have in common

Night on or at night
No light to lead us
Every random path appears
In disrepair, daymares crouched
Behind each mossy stump
Reaching out, out
And death the only thing
We have in common

Upreach or reach in
Only the untouchable
Star to guide the lost
Who wander, not north
Or south but only
Up into an unknown
Sky or down into the sea
Following a voice that cries
Come home, my child
Come home

— *Charles Watts*

What Have I Learned About Love?

Well for starters, it's a messy drug
And there's all kinds of forms of it
Friends, family, pets
But the one we most commonly find ourselves addicted to
Is romance

And why is that

Could it simply be our nature
Or perhaps nurture
Or both

Does our unconditional connection to other human beings
Wish that we simultaneously share this experience of life
together

Or are we just doing what mommy and daddy did
What our uncles and aunts taught us

Are we replicating what they had
Or chasing a dream that we lack

Were they perfect example of an idea
Or just the blueprint on heartache

Are we fantasizing about fulfilling a fairytale
Or merely trying to fill a void
That was never quite occupied by an absent mother
or neglectful father

Or maybe
It has nothing to do with them at all

Maybe it's the thrill of it

The ups and downs of emotions

The opening of h e a r t s and slamming of doors

The melding of minds

The r o l l e r c o a s t e r of adventure!

          Oh, and don't even get me started
          On well, ya know

That spot behind his ear
          That tickle on her neck
The taste of his lips
          The warmth of her breath
Skin to skin
          Soul to soul
Passionate
          Naked
Completely whole

Oh how *electrifying* to see such sparks flying

To feel two worlds colliding
As the universe makes s p a c e

For a moment so timeless
A life so vibrant
A love so pure
It's almost impossible to distinguish reality

Til you realize

It's the source of
Reality

Our existence

The reason you and I are here
Why we pick up a glass and cheer
Why we clap and dance and forget our fears
And just

Be

But hey, who am I to tell you what it is
Nothing more than a single perspective

So, I dare you

Go out and try it for yourself
Find as much of it as you can
And soak it up however you need to

With a partner, a companion, or on your own
But most of all, please embrace it
Fight with it, lose it, then find it again

Because through all that
Joy, abundance, and turmoil
I'm still asking myself

What Have I Learned About Love

— *Christian Morant*

Overloaded

I tried to be tied down
But couldn't quite figure out
What I really wanted out of life
So I shut down
Abandoned everybody who trust me
And tried to love me
Cuz I couldn't bear the thought of them
Knowing that I was strugglin'
Mentally, financially,
And everything else in between
As pride got the best of me
Tempted me and then tested me
By asking my ego
What kind of evil makes a lesser me
Then using that knowledge
With full intention to make a mess of me
Embarrassing to say the least
Having to cope with everything
On your own inside your dome
Feeling like you're so alone
But never wanna rock the boat
So you do your best to hold
It all together
Til one day you explode
From emotion overload
Airing out your whole soul
And bearing down to the bone
Where you're finally exposed
To be the human
That you've been pursuing all along
As you hid behind a monster
So he could write some songs

Turning rights into wrongs
And replacing your thoughts
With a little idea
That you don't belong
Like what's the point of livin'
When you've already given up
On everybody in your life
That you ever claimed to love...

Well, I'll tell you what the point is
No more avoidance
Time to stand up and speak out
For the voiceless
For those who feel joyless
For those who feel poisoned
For those who feel like they're trapped
And have no other choices
But to work and be slave
Fake a smile and behave
While the money that you make
Goes to someone else's bank
So they can live happy lives
Off your efforts and your time
Til you're no longer needed
Then they simply cut your ties
Like a puppet, they say fuck it
Use you then kick your bucket
As they throw you out
With the bathwater like you're nothin'
But the bottom of a barrel
So you go and grab a barrel
Making sure to grip it tight
As the muzzle meets your temple
Cuz they got you going mental
Thinking that you're worthless

Hoping that the metal's
Gonna solve all your burdens
When all it's gonna do
Is leave your loved ones hurtin'
So I'm here to beg you
To stay determined
To live a better life
To ignore all the lies
To put down the bottle
Step away from the knife
To look deep inside
And try to realize
That each and every single one of us
Deserves
                to
                        survive

— *Christian Morant*

Runaway

I should have run away with you
Instead I ran away from you
Like a train off its tracks
Unhinged, I turned my back
Out of control, spiraling
Your sight of me, frightening
This side of me you finally see
This monster I'm ashamed to be
And to think you once loved this creature
For all my loco—motives and imperfected features
My flaws and disasters, a derailing chapter
Of life where you only mattered
But gave it all up to be a fuckin rapper!
When you're the one I should have chased after
A dream I can't unshatter
But hope to one day claim a new fate
And wash away the pain
As we simply
      run
           away

— *Christian Morant*

Hospice

My granddad's in a prison
Otherwise known as the system
Or what y'all call a hospital
But only two of us can visit
Which is kinda odd if you think about it
Cuz I would wanna be surrounded
By all those who love me
And want nothing more than to hug me
As they show affection and be the reflection
That he was for those I can't mention
And everybody else around the world
Where he built a genuine connection
By embracing the gift he was given
An entertainer with a wealth of wisdom
Sharing everything he learned about life
To anyone willing to listen
To the message between the melodies
To the rhythm between every beat
To that feeling that you get in your soul
When your favorite song comes on the radio
Cuz that's what it's all about
Music that brings the best out
In all of us
            So no matter what you're going through
                    Don't forget
            There's always time
                    to crank up
                            the tunes

— *Christian Morant*

Loved You Better

I wish I would have loved you better
I wish that I would have never
Lied to you, tried to hide the truth
Especially after chance number two
Where you let me in, shared me with friends
Believed I wouldn't do this shit again
But lo and behold wouldn't you know
Went right back to being an asshole
Taking for granted a beautiful soul
Shattering the heart that made me whole
Giving up everything just so I could feel
Like I'm at the top of the totem pole
As you watched me crash and burn
Asking how I could be so absurd
Wondering what it will take for me
To open my mind and finally learn
How to treat a woman with respect
Which is what you deserve in the end
Not someone who's gonna go out of their way
To make you a victim of all of their mess
Make you a casualty of a train wreck
Make you the sadness that you've ever been
Not even upset, just disappointed
That you put your faith in anything I said
That you opened your home with open arms
That you shared pieces with me others harmed
That you introduced me to your whole family
Just so they can see how deep of a scar
I would leave on their little girl
The only one willing to give the world
To someone like me, the same human being
Who took advantage of
            such a
            remarkable   QUEEN

— *Christian Morant*

48

How (Not) to Write a Cover Letter, a Step-By-Step Guide – Addressed to No One

Step one: Wait until T-minus 1.25 hours before deadline to even start.

Step two: Attach it to something you very recently said wasn't ready.

Step three: Completely disregard the formalities of cover letters.

Step four: Address it to no one, certainly not To Whom It May Concern.

Step five: Trust in your voice to speak loud enough to pique intrigue without context.

— *Cory Stegelin*

a new america

"i pledge allegiance, to the flag,
of the united states of america.
and to the republic, for which it stands
one nation, under god, indivisible,
with liberty and justice for all."

liberty is a confusing word
it seems a simple right we all obtain
but a phenomenon only a few attain in life
since 1776 this nation has preached of freedom
and liberty for all from the talons of oppression
only to recreate new systems of oppression themselves
up north we learned about the history of injustice
we talked of the discrimination of the past
how we have supposedly grown
beyond oppression and into complete liberty
but reality means trapping our own citizens
under the systematic punishments of identity
our policing system that exists to protect us
harms more than it protects
disproportionately targeting our citizens of color
state-sanctioned violence
spills blood into our city streets
as voices echo through alleyways to honor those fallen
only to be shuffled back into cages themselves
abraham lincoln was supposed to release the shackles
that held black americans captive from life
only to segregate them to the outskirts of society
mass incarceration a rebirth of these shackles
black men are carted into prisons by the thousands
for crimes white americans commit too
but for white america
a crime is not a crime but a mistake
a mistake they need to learn from
not by locking them inside a cage

but rather to set them free
back into the world only to commit the crimes again
our nation exists in a limbo
between claiming superiority
and emerging as the laughing stock of the globe
a pandemic hits the world
and we claim we've got it under control
we're trapped inside our houses for over a year
only leaving to hide our faces from friends
and family in isolation
protecting our neighbors and fellow citizens
viewed as a threat to our freedom
we continue to long for normalcy and the past
but never work to restore what once was
up north we hide behind masks of inclusion and equity
to speak behind their backs of others
unworthiness to live
down south an exterior of
"southern hospitality and comfort"
the same gossip of oppression of those we call friends
love is but a fleeting feeling that few experience
even when found we cannot express it
hiding behind closed doors, the only truly free space
the space where i can love a woman,
and maybe a man too
years of concealing my identity
among a mask of the status quo
emerge as a proud bisexual woman of color
watch the nation destroy that pride
and shatter it to shreds
i weep for the future of this nation i call home
i fear for the state of the country that claims superiority
i struggle to find pride in nationality and citizenship
a so called new america emerges
but merely exists as the same america
that left my ancestors shackled in chains of oppression

— *Emily Wingfield*

an afternoon on sullivan's island

i connect with an old friend.
i absorb the conversations like the raven
hair upon my head absorbs the sun. what more
could my soul need within this moment?
from shore to shore we closed the distance
with sand dollars and ocean waves.
the smell of sunscreen and salted air
makes one blue smell together.
sit upon the sand and dig away
our worries of future, friends, and foes
until we reach the core
holding our suffering deeply and with care.
emotions swim through our veins
and weave our minds together.
he found a living sand dollar
in the sand beneath his feet.
it reminds us of life
each inhale and exhale to follow.
pure and simple in nature.
here alone with a friend
whose home is no longer near
but whose heart i packed with me to move.
the ocean is calm,
resting sheaths of water upon our skin.
the world could swallow the whole of me
and i wouldn't bat an eye.

— *Emily Wingfield*

listening to garden song by phoebe bridgers while laying in bed

i dream of life
upon the hills
eternal & poetic

watch my feet
sink further
beneath the soil

fly from the edge
of abridged hope
above the water

a cushion resting
against blue walls
i trap myself inside

i don't know more
than life upon a hill
in your garden

awake at last
beneath her leaves
breathe life in me

— *Emily Wingfield*

ode to lavinia fisher and other ghostly friends

lavinia fisher lies
near the old city jail
she shared your message
with the devil
lept from the gallows
to the snapped neck
of highway robber turned serial killer

ghostly apparitions are not
something to fear
friends in lonely places

circular congregation church
photoshoot in a graveyard
a stroll down philadelphia alley
book yourself a room
in the mills house hotel
so you can host
a tea party with your ghostly friends

ghostly apparitions are not
something to fear
but friends in lonely places

— *Emily Wingfield*

someday soon

you sit down in the shower
sink into fear
exploited for their benefit
just another zombie of the world
discarded among the rest
in a world gone shallow
oppression rushes
through city streets
capitalism!
full of screams and hope
few things more dangerous
than man and greed
bleed down your back
there's little left
inside this body
flaunt my open wounds
murder my dreams
bury them in a hole
beneath the earth
feel the creatures eat away
should i be writing this?
they have it worse
stop trying to become a star
sink back down
into anonymity
wait forever day to day
just to die
someday soon

— *Emily Wingfield*

Pink: Chiquimula, Guatemala

I
They speak, and the syllables
splash into their saucepans
like fish, wet and sizzling,
plump-scaled, pink-scaled,
gunky fins and flanks that drip
with balls of sweat and salt.

The *niñas chiquitas* giggle
when I place my hand on the
bubbling stovetop—when I squeal
and lurch backwards, pink flesh
pulsing, cheeks streaked
with soot and humiliation.

!Mira la gringa! I can still feel
my heartbeat in my fingertips,
but they slap me on the back
and dip my hand in the
water basin, wrapping it with
stiff strips of tape, grinning
as we toss our tortillas.

II
I see a stump of bone, a slab
of pink muscle and flesh,
crusted dry, flaking and peeling
around her kneecap—a splash
of blood, a speckle of ash.

She swats at the flies that
settle in the mush of the wound,
sighing and blotting her forehead,
blinking at the ants in the dirt
by her bare feet. *El hospital
está demasiado lejos*, she breathes.
(The hospital is too far).
Y nadie podía llevarme.

III
I swing the purse over my
shoulder and lug my suitcase
through the gray-carpet terminal—
air conditioning and peanut
packets, mayonnaise and
stale onion rings.

I set my passport on my lap
and unbuckle the leather wings,
tapping the page with the
rectangular stamp—pink and
smudged around the edges,
glaring like a wound.

Guatemala.
Departed.
17.June.2018.

— *Evangelne Sanders*

Death According to Michael

10:47 p.m.
Heart twitching in the hospital bed,
staggered slurps and beeps
like chirps strung from a robin's beak,
monitor line jagged and red,
jagged and flat.

> *10:47 p.m.*
> He steps into the garden,
> the gushing gates, the bushes
> and berries and spattered greens
> of moss-soaked streets,
> of white-walled tunnels and tapestries.

10:48 p.m.
Shooting like the sun
when they slap static onto his chest,
squeezing and slinging the breaths
from his cavity—coughing,
spluttering, as he tips into
open-eyed death.

And I´m still waiting, he tells me.
Waiting for what? I ask.

*To close my eyes
and live again.*

— *Evangelne Sanders*

When You Don't Have Ankles (Taylor's Poem)

She stores her left foot
in a pull-out freezer
beside a bag of frozen peas.

The black garbage bag
(INFECTIOUS WASTE: DANGER)
rustles as she peels back
skins of plastic, tilts
the foot into the frame
of the camera. Strips
of tape and fabric
strap around the line
of the lower leg,
creased at the joints—
latex-blue cloth, stiff,
puckered like a cold pack.
I see the L-shape of the foot,
the ankle, the jutting bone
of the lower calf.

She stores her right foot
on a desk in her room,
plastered bones stacked
into a skeleton statue.

She had wired the little toes
together, shoved a needle
through the shaft
of the marrow, smeared

the disks and pellets
with super glue.

*

She shuffles through the door
with a smile and sits
in the front row,
hooking her backpack
to her chair. She twists
around to face the class.
I got some shoes yesterday,
she says, pointing at the
red-and-white Converse
with bright rubber soles.

They're male shoes, actually.

*Shopping is hard
when you don't have ankles.*

— *Evangelne Sanders*

The Book of Christopher

He picked crumbs
from the folds
of his sweatpants,
bread wad clumped like paste
in his cheek,
water-white eyes—
blue flecks and swirls
wedged into glass marbles.
Skin: cream from a tube,
curdled sheep milk.

He said he summoned
storms with the sap
of the Holy Spirit (he chewed
the Bible verses
and spat them onto the
cement. Crusted teeth,
caked with sugar).
He said he predicted
the patterns of planets
and celestial bodies—flicked
stars into the sky,
clipped them
to a clothesline.

Miracles. Nothing
but miracles. Nothing
without miracles.

I can still see it: the way
he sighed, shook his
head, stood

to brush the dust
from his sandals

before leaving
without
a
word.

— *Evangelne Sanders*

The Saxophonist (Feat. His Three Vehicles)

Jazz is a steamship.

The brassy spit and shriek, the copper
stench of sweat and horn, clunky valves

and steaming coils of pipework, oil
ducts and boiling water—a golden factory,

a sweltering patch, a crack of yellow
blood (crackling fire) in the skin.

Jazz is a race car.

Foot pedals pressed like gas pedals,
black-and-white checkered flags and

streaks of skid marks and dirt, flapping
wrists, a flash of teeth and metal.

Jazz is a limousine.

Crisp cotton handcuffs, velvet and
purple gowns, velvet and burgundy

rolls of carpets, a rippling smile and
black-cherry lips.

> And as he smashes the valves with shaking
> fingers—brown cheeks puffing, pulsing—
>
> as I watch the folds of his chin, the cracks
> in his sagging eyelids, the drops of saliva

and sweat on the slab of his nose, I sense
my strange body: perched in the passenger

seat, bag clutched to my chest, blinking
out the window to the gray hills—eternally

in transit.

— *Evangelne Sanders*

Dewberries

Each autumn I yank out
the vines, declare I don't
care if no berries appear
the following year. Yet no matter
how many brambles I remove,

more pop up. And every spring
I'm back in my Lowcountry garden
picking dewberries tight, or plump,
with sweet-tart, black-red juice—
fruit sure to qualify as superfood.

Today I reach across prodigious
oak logs beginning to decay
in the spot where the arborist crew
left them after the last hurricane.
I startle a broad-headed skink and

it startles me. Hurrying away, it
tunnels through a chamber of vines.
Calming myself, I pick every ripe
berry I find. I'll salve scratched arms
tonight and tomorrow morning I'll

make dewberry syrup, drizzle it on
buttery crepes, while somewhere
outside the skink swallows moths
and bugs, and everywhere
dewberries produce new shoots.

— *Frances J. Pearce*

Stranded at the Open Mic

Sipping tepid tea, I listen
to you speak your poems

of loneliness. Through
the plate glass window

behind you, I see lightning
writhe across the night.

Then comes rain slapping
scorched pavement.

Soon water will obliterate
the usual roadways.

I haven't a boat, only a car
parked five blocks away,

where my bumbershoot
now resides. I'm wearing

fine leather sandals instead
of tall rubber boots. The skirt

of my white dress is like
a moonflower unfurling.

Your resonant voice floods
the café, even as individual words

attempt to hide. I shut my eyes,
capitulate to the storm outside.

— *Frances J. Pearce*

A Poem in Which I Explicate My Nose

(after Danez Smith)

Nase. (German word for nose. Through my orphaned grandmother, I might be as much as one-quarter German.)

Pointy. (As in "blue-eyed soul sister with the pointy nose," even though my eyes are mocha brown.)

Ski jump. (Wait. No. That was Richard Nixon.)

Garden of blackheads.

Accidental target of a softball bat.

Why we were best friends. (Hers even more enormous than mine.)

An important part of my face.

A bit longer than my father's, a bit shorter than my mother's.

Chute for snot.

Gateway to my lungs.

Indispensable.

— *Frances J. Pearce*

A War Against Solace

The drywall hears my sobs
Hushed whimpers to vehement weeping
And the hardwood catches my tears
One
       by
            one
                  by
                        one

They bind my edges
As I lay out all the pieces of my soul
As I search for glue to fix what's been broken
I can only trust my own trembling hands

I pray this room is fortified enough
To keep away anyone kind enough
To approach while I'm defenseless
I can't bear the weight of their love in this state

My hands have cuts
From the jagged edges of my fragmented self
But I can't accept gloves from anyone
My damage, my responsibility

Yet I forgot to lock the door
And the floors have made space for one more
My sobs are louder
And the walls refuse to hold them in

Someone else is running it all
She's young and doesn't shy away from helplessness
Instead she bawls and bawls
Until someone's love hears her grief

Until there's another set of hands
Unarmed and ready to be maimed
By all my agony
Unintimidated by how long this project might take

I try to call upon my cell
To keep her out
But her courage has yet to be broken
And there's extraordinary strength in her youth

She kicks down the door
And takes a sledgehammer to the walls
She makes as much noise as she can
So solace can't pretend not to hear her

I'm weak without my isolation
And must wave a white flag
Her spirit is victorious
As is all the love she has called upon

— *Gracie Bell*

At the Waterfront

The notes of the saxophone drifted down the dock
Blending with the waves rippling on shore
Chilly winds brushed our cheeks
And we loved the excuse to sit extra close

As we silently watched the sailboat glide by
Our interlaced fingers hidden in her sweater sleeve
Laughter hung in the air
Children's giggles and elder's chuckles

Oh how I longed to kiss her
Amidst the chaotic serenity
But hate could be lurking in the crowd
And I feared its retaliation

So instead we sat gazing at one another
Finding peace in the simplicity of a Friday afternoon
Dreaming of a day when fright had no place in our
hearts
And hatred had no place in theirs

— *Gracie Bell*

Until

I had never found comfort in intimacy
I had never found warmth or laughter
Never found care or concern

I had only ever found objectification in intimacy
I had only ever found disdain and contempt
Only ever found fear and dread

Until I laid naked in her bed as she counted my freckles
      Seventeen
        Eighteen
          Nineteen

Until our bare legs were intertwined
with wine glasses in our hands
      Cheers to being with a woman
        Cheers to vulnerability
          Cheers to dancing in our underwear

Until we fell asleep pressed together
      Hearts beating slower
        Drifting into dreams
          Dreams of one another

— *Gracie Bell*

For Those Who Grieve

We all want a forever
A forever happiness
A forever love

But it seems as though this doesn't exist
Distance grows silently between us
Crawling within the cracks in the foundation
Until the relationship crumbles down

Sometimes though we almost get a forever
But then there is our everlasting enemy: death
A very fickle thing
For sometimes we see it from miles away
Other times it creeps around a corner and silently
snatches our most beloved

Fret not my dear friend because this
does not mean it is all pointless
We receive bits of other souls with
every connection we make
These pieces plant themselves deep within us
They grow and they flourish
Until we are made up of many individuals

These traits, these memories are what give us forever
I heed the counsel of my late grandpa before I ask the
wrong person for advice
I am reminded of my first love every time I
 eat a clementine
I follow the words of my high school mentor
when I find myself without optimism
I possess a fondness for writing
because of a particular english teacher

Relationships that no longer exist
People that are no longer around
Continue to mold my being and expand my soul
Their roots intertwined with the fabric of my existence

We all want a forever
But instead life is made up of tiny eternities
Dynamic moments that are everlasting

— *Gracie Bell*

Love Dark

There were no stars when I first saw her:
she glistened asteroid, obsidian, dark matter.

The jealous heart small in my chest drowned
in the dew of her clavicle, philtrum, suprasternal notch.
Better not to swim there in growing thirst.

Tart light spooled in eyes just-ripened oranges,
with one hand I could tear her flooding apart.
Andromeda, may I invite collision?

Let me string for you rogue planets
to hang about your neck, droplets
visible only in infrared. Let me be your clasp.

It was dark when first I saw her, therefore
it was dark, deepest hottest dark,
when I began to breathe in space.

— *Hailey Williams*

Rain-Bringer

Some blue withered thing comes to your field,
scrapes paws at the water pump, drinks.
"Better cut down that sun" it smiles,
shoulders aquiver it turns the crank.

Water spills and clouds put out the sun
which rolls to its feet. it drinks and grows strong.
Around your tabby-walled barn dark wind spins.
Your well's gone dry, shadows stretch long,

not a drop for your field till it reawakens.
Dried tobacco hangs like ears above you
thumb the pale pebble of the sun.

it appears so thin it could be smoked,
takes the sun flat in palm and skips true
across the sky (who cries) and all is done.

— *Hailey Williams*

Reunion

I pull from tangled
island ventricles
pale claws nearly dust
to stash in my breast pocket.
Clittering china, I picture
a family of crab ghosts converging
over my pulse, ready to tuck
into their first bloody meal after death;
eye stalks sway in synchrony
raised in prayer to Sea, or
perhaps his brother, Sky.
Spectres Crustacea
mingling in my pocket,
I scoop out my heart
and permit you to feast.

— *Hailey Williams*

Tribute to Praxiteles' Aphrodite of Knidos

1.   Woman
Did her hair curl & fists knot,
were her legs pale & slender
perfect tendons in a quiver,
or dense & dark like toasted honey?

Did her smile fade / flood, like
wind-carried lyre on hoar-frost night,
or teeth like moths in filmy light?
Was she woman as well as stone?

2.   Sculpture
Did she hold her earth-hot tears
in quarry-belly, until Praxiteles
rewrote Aphrodite's birth of sea,
marble > foam for immortality?

Is she unperturbed that her neck broke,
all those Olympian lovers croaked &
her kingdom tore out its own throat?
Did she ever learn to sigh?

— *Hailey Williams*

Amphibious

He meets me at the bridge
and tells me to discard
my scales. Urgently: he says
it's time for me to join him above.
It's simple, he says,
just pull them out
like so many fingernails.

He does not have them,
so he does not know.
He's given me no clippers;
I dig and rip from the root.
It takes hours.

He grows bored, drowses
beneath tupelo. My blood
stains the swamp,
bubbles in my wounds.
I'm cleansed by tannin water.
My ribs and thighs shredded,
oozing, I roll onto the riverbank.
He gathers me up in the net of his arms.

He has a place for me,
a nice home. I'll have someone
to look after each day.
There is awe in his eyes.
I have hidden my gills;
I hope that as I learn to breathe
his air, they do not fall away.

— *Hailey Williams*

December 21st, 2019, At the Dentist

It's the end of the year
And I'm aware of my teeth.
Mouth stretched from the leverage of a mirror,
The low gurgle of saliva sucked up,
The scrape of steel on plaque,
Build to a respect for things cavernous.

At solstice the dentist's light
Finds the gap between teeth
And a spot on the wall
Of the mouth is illuminated.

You'd almost expect to find a painting there.
Maybe an antelope dotted white during a chant
Or a mammoth, mystic smears for luck
On a hunt that will end in rain
And a curse skyward for the betrayal
Of wet fur and an empty mouth.

Things within resist cleaning:
Caves, the hollows where light
Is musty and candles burn like wet cigarettes.
But in the flickering, an occasional shape
Perhaps a wall and we turn instinctively to avoid it.
The steps echo, the next mixing with all the rest
And someone asks "Where are we going?"
Turn around and for all we know we've gone nowhere
Or we've gone everywhere
Lost in our darkness.

— *Harold Oberman*

Garden Poem, Charleston Carriage House May 2020

Back behind the main house
Down the driveway,
Outside of where euphemistic horses stayed
Lays my garden of gravel and leaves.
No soil sees sunlight there.

Owners ignored this plot
And I too, quarantined in inaction.
Instead of a rake, instead of a sign,
I look out the window, pick up a pen
And muse on what it can't undo.

Strange art this gardening within:
Grow meaning from never marched ground,
Shed light on silent dirt.

— *Harold Oberman*

After the Cooper River Bridge Run, 2019

Thirty-thousand over the bridge to the line.
Miles and times ticked off in splits
Until under the banner it ends.

They'll wear their numbers for hours
Bobby-pinned singlets stuck to their skin.
On the peninsula they'll linger
Chirping outside cafes midmorning
Dabbing sports drinks and mimosas
Content and courseless pigeons
       Crumb-struck, sidewalk fed.
Watches stopped, pocketed,
Finish times a flightless wing.

The sun rises to zenith:
Overhead and noon the shadows upright and within the body.
But soon, the relentless descent to evening.
Last lean at the line as the day ends
Shadows stretch to the tape
Darkness ever-longer and overlapping
Until time and night consume the race.

— *Harold Oberman*

Where the Keys Go

Somewhere in the endless underthings of a house
Where dust dares not move
And fly wings crisp,
It might be the curtained sill corner with webs
Or the place roaches scuttle when lights click on,
Even under a drawerful of change,
Somewhere,
They're having a party.

The jingle of small talk,
Of the day's duties –
"Damn back lock's sticking again."
"Crazy sonofabitch stuck me upside down in the ignition."
"I wish I could rattle that tyke just once." --
Rises to ringing half beyond audible.

A slender brown Webster is tipsy
Talks of the time before he was copied
Staggers backwards and says he is happy
Traces the rim of his glass.

In a corner, talk turns to things important.
A trunk key responds to a skeleton key,
"Chains? Rings? I say they're the same."
A master key scoffs at the irony of his name.
Another misquotes Marx.

It's like a scene from late night cable nobody cares to see,
Bit actors involved in plots as thick as Three-In-One oil,
But the key to it is this:
They might turn up when they damn well please,
Right under your nose and you'll swear you've already looked there.
Look again. You can't keep your keys in your pocket.

— *Harold Oberman*

On a Bench, At the Battery, March 2020

It's just out of range, that conversation.
Snippets, high pitched giggles and laughter.
They all had something important to say, did they not?
They all had something important to say.

But those words were not meant for my ear,
Nor yours, and that's the beauty of it.
It rose like a Spring tide spilling over the seawall
And receded leaving only puddles
For what we imagined they said:
Something glistening; Something reflective;
Something so blue it makes you gasp.

— *Harold Oberman*

The Woman
Who Raised Me

Her name was Sheila Smith
She was from Detroit
One of 12
And had a rose stick n poke tattoo
On her right ankle
that she gave herself
with a sewing needle and ink
during her high school lunch period

Every Summer she took me fishing
For Cat Fish
At this little pond by the Montgomery airport

We'd hop in her van
which smelled of pork rinds
and Glade air fresheners
and drive down the back Alabama highways

Stopping only once
at a little road side stand along the way
to buy a bucket of worms
to use for bait
and a pound of boiled peanuts
to eat while we fished

I'd wait there next to her
as she laughed with the guy behind the stand
My 8-year-old bare feet
Frying on the August asphalt
so hot it almost felt cold

we sat out there for hours
cracking the peanuts
wiping the sweat from our necks
baiting the hooks

until we finally caught enough
to feed the whole neighborhood

Once the heat began to sink into the ground
where it radiated off the blades of grass
and the sun became a red orange orb
slowly slipping into the horizon

We'd head back into town
the sound of cicadas guiding us
as we drove in silence
to Sheila's house
where she'd fry up our day's bounty
encrusted in flower and bred crumbs

the grease popping off the cast iron skillet
and the smoke filling the kitchen air
a blue Kool-Aid Burst in hand
to wash down the salty sweaty heat of late afternoon
while the neighborhood kids ran around me
in one laughter filled blur

— *Jean Catherine Hubbard*

I Don't Like the Beach but I Love You

I could sit in silence with you
as you eat your egg sandwich
on the beach
and the seagulls flock and laugh
for an eternity

Lie in the shoreline of the ocean
and let the tide lap gently
over our limp bodies

arms spread out in the wet sand
as if the world of fellow beach goers around us
has simply vanished
and it's just us
and the force of the ocean

you told me thank you
for joining you in your happy place
but you have no idea
how wonderful it is
to meet you here

— *Jean Catherine Hubbard*

Nana's Seafood and Soul

It was Saturday
In May

The rain finally stopped
And we emerged from bed
Drenched in sex and draped in sheets
Just in time for the golden hue
Of late afternoon

We ventured out into the city
For crab legs from Nana's
Where we waited in line with the other locals
Humming and bustling and chatting
And laughing
We carried our bounty home as we walked the streets
The sky turning pink

It was us against the flies
As we sat on the porch and devoured
Fingers and face covered in juice
From the fresh meat of the LowCountry

Just the two of us
Swatting the flies
Stealing glances
And laughing

— *Jean Catherine Hubbard*

kitchen sink

I brushed my teeth
In your kitchen sink

Made certain not to get any toothpaste
On the clean dishes I washed for you
When your brain was too scattered
To do so yourself

"Oh you don't have to do that"
"I don't mind"

I'll always wash the dishes
You leave in the kitchen sink
If you'll sing for me while you shower

— *Jean Catherine Hubbard*

Henrietta

"Oh Clark, I'm so sorry"
Hushed voices ushered me into
The realm of consciousness
Where last night's indulgence
Slowly churned into that morning's regret

No one needed to tell me
I already knew from the words
That crept into my little sister's bedroom
Where I laid on her pink fairy sheets
Foggy brained and void of dignity

My grandmother was dead

The last words I spoke of her
While she was still alive
And desperately clinging to life
Were that she was a cunt
A cockroach that would never die

Pent up resentment for all
That she had put us through
All that we endured at the hands
Of her callous grip
Spewed out of me with the aid
Of an aged tawny port

How was I to know that this time
Was actually the last
For there were countless calls
Before this one
Countless drunken late night dials
Before this final plea for help

But this one was different
Because her lips were blue

My brother's words played in my head
Long after her last breath
"Jean, her lips are blue"
Her lips are blue
Her lips are blue
And surely
I'm going to hell

— *Jean Catherine Hubbard*

We All Go A Little

I'm fed up with this straight boy who knows
what he's got going on. How to hold it.
How to pack the padded back of pants he picks.

Loose fit that falls, hangs, caught. Arched stretch
to air belly hairs. A path like a magnet, like a tractor beam
or a promise he won't keep. Why not

pull the string that swings beneath the single bulb?
Let them bounce, the shadows in the valleys of his flesh.
Let them oscillate while the light spins.

Taxidermy corpse on a swivel chair,
Vera Miles to my Tony Perkins in a dress,
in a blanket round my shoulders like a shawl.

My superimposed and toothy grin. And, when
I am finally found out, when, somewhere in another room
on the other side of dappled glass, he listens—like a child

scolded for scaring their mother with a near
miss—to someone telling him of his own
near miss, when he dodged my eye contact

the third and fourth times, the way the clock's steady step
falters. First: heartbeat skip, sick stomach twist and then:
me, harmless in a wooden chair. Or maybe I'm the fly

I wouldn't harm. I crawl around on the hand, unaware
of the threat, grateful just to be and to be left alone.
A car dredged from the swamp.

— *John Luke Byrne*

The runners have already started taking off their shirts

and their shorts are still short,
riding high on their bare thighs.
One just ran past me on the bench.

His laborious breath, his reddened chest
giving off a light glisten. He's only
just removed his shirt, maybe,

before rounding the corner toward me,
tucked it into his waistband at the back: gray
cotton gone grayer with the damp

under a cloud-gray sky. And, of course,
the whole of it is still bodily, all muscled
arms and thumping legs on the graveled path,

feet crunching as he runs, panting, past,
within feet of me, and I have enough
time to think of other things that come

within touching distance of one another—
the sky that drops low to stroke the horizon
and the horizon holding it up, or words

that fumble toward their clumsy meaning
and the meaning trying to catch them as they fall.
Even what appears to touch does not—still: space,

empty if we don't fill it. Azaleas are still in bloom,
exploding over their bushes for these few weeks.
How many has this runner seen as he traverses streets

now nearly deserted? I'm letting things go lately,
but I will never be finished with desire,
how different I feel on either end

of its covetous lens. Though
most often I'm on both ends, like now,
as my eyes strain to take in the whole

abundance of him, the hairs on his body
sticking to him, the way his lungs fill
and empty, the trickle of sweat in his armpits,

the scandalous bounce at his crotch, and still
I have just enough time to check my own
posture, to smooth my own hair and put on

an inscrutable scowl, like, if he wanted to,
he could find an excuse to stop and talk to me—
ask for directions? Pick up an item of mine

I could conveniently drop in time for him
to come to my rescue?—and I could pretend
to see through the charade and not care

because it's so much a part of living
to want and be wanted and want to be.
But, also, and of course, he's already past,

and I'm still on the bench, extending the moment
long enough to imagine it was significant
for both of us, as if I'm not better suited

to fossilize here with an arm outstretched
after something, a statue with mouth half opened

as if saying come back, please, let me touch you,

or maybe just taking in a breath.

— *John Luke Byrne*

French Gay Bar, at Pentacost

An old man tells dirty jokes, but means nothing
by them. We like him, like the history he brings
to our long low table in our own dark upper room.

How to explain the complexities of a heart
both open and closed across the barrier
between two mother tongues? Alexandre asks

if I've ever been in love, and I can answer him
honestly. I Doubting Thomas my way through
the conversation, though it has less to do with doubt

than with how quickly the subjects come and go.
I keep up with what's been said, but scarcely have time
for rebuttal. And we're all waiting here anyway

for proof of what we've been whispering to ourselves
while walking down this city's lonely stone alleys
on Thursday nights so late they're Friday mornings.

Tonight I skip the bus and let myself be driven
home by a stranger. In the back seat, Alexandre
holds my hand in silence, and I feel the Spirit

spread through me, filling me up. Is there a tongue
of flame as confirmation? I know I will not sleep.
I want this day's late fire to burn itself

to cinders, want my clothes drying on the line
in the living room to smell of woodsmoke by morning.
Tomorrow, yes, tomorrow I will spread the good news,

tomorrow I will wear a badge of truth and speak

in tongues to the masses at the metro stop
at St. Anne's and they will hear and understand

and they will be filled with the same sustaining
substance, something that straddles joy and satisfaction,
the same sensation I have now, standing at the stoop

of my host mom's house, not yet ready to go in,
not ready to fake sleep, not ready for this feeling
to fade, to fizzle, as I know it will, as it always does.

— *John Luke Byrne*

Unrequited Evening with One of Poseidon's Lesser Sons

I watch him shed his exomis
from the pristine curves
of his river-smoothed body. Linen,
once taut, now worn to gauzy holes
his skin winks through. Like barnacles
affixed to his vessel's bowed bottom
I cannot unfasten my eyes
from the hollow of his neck, flecked
with the bristles of a clean shave
at midday; nor the line that slopes
from the tips of his fingers to the balls
of his pointed feet; nor the arch
of his spine as he plunges headlong
into the sea's golden blue. Bathed in spray,
I want to cling to him like the red
mullet slime on his fishing line,
forgotten, cast aside for a brief respite
from late summer's hot sun; I want to coat
his skin like the fine layer of caked dust
the salt has only just started to lick
away. Daylight ripples across his surfaces,
across his fibers impossibly thin.

Sundown now and cicadas sing
from tamarisk trees, bursting with pink flowers
like his tongue on which he's placed one
of Meleager's shrill-voiced insects—a testament
to his inherited bull-like boldness. He wags it
in my direction, sheer goofiness, or maybe
just to show me the inside of his mouth.

Eyes on him, shallow as a puddle,
bottomless as the depths he dives, and here,
beside him, I am a fingered string
of tactile pearls, the way sea foam like soap swirls,
one of his girls. I am the singer on his tongue,
flicked free, so he can swallow.

— *John Luke Byrne*

Crescendo Decrescendo Diminuendo

Today the twitching muscle
finally twists. Outstretched hand
finds something to grasp and the gasping
mouth lets out a sound.

In the end, I am
the action that slams the door
or hammers in the nail.

No more sustained, suspended endings.
No matter where, or when, the sun sets
eventually. The day becomes That Day.
Early to earlier. Later to now to then.

Give me sunset. Give me moonrise.
Give me high tide and dishes
dried with a towel, stacked
in their place on the shelf, and clothes
unclipped from the line, folded,
to be transferred, later,
to the drawer.

Even out the ground floor window
of my childhood bedroom, there is
a last escape. Even when again
becomes again again. There will be an end.

Today I let the timer drop
to zero and then when it rings
I wind it back up and whistle
while it ticks. Today it finally clicks.

You start the count-
down—I'll be the basket
at the buzzer. I'll be touch-
down. I'll be lift-off and landing.

I still cast quiet spells on airplanes
and long drives. Miles between words
I speak aloud. Is the ending when the magic

stopped or only when I noticed? My first
kiss under moonlight marked the end
of my lips not knowing other lips.
I thought I knew that then.

— *John Luke Byrne*

a room for everyone

so many spirits
alas, St. Peter
so many souls

"where were you when it happened?"
"Washington, DC, and you?"
"Memphis, Tennessee"

bodies segregated,
a room for everyone
impossible,
there are too many

"how did it happen?"
"i was enjoying a play, an exceptionally good play i might add
my wife was seated next to me in the balcony
back of the head over my right ear,
never saw it coming
they said it was from a Derringer pistol,
it's of no consequence"

larger rooms?
everyone with the same surname?
too confusing

"i had just stepped out of my motel room,
on my way to support striking sanitation workers
through my right cheek, smashed my jaw,
down my spinal cord and lodged in my shoulder
praise the Lord,
never saw it coming either
i was told it was from a Remington 760 Gamemaster
whatever that is"

hair color, religious denomination, sexual deviants,
skin color, accumulated wealth, bigotry?
stereotypes must be employed,
there is no other way...

How You Met Your Demise Rooms

a drowning room, the suicide room,
a still born room, the choked on a chicken bone room,
got thrown from a horse room, a cholera room,
the Bubonic plaque room, the pandemic room,
an assassination room

"well, it looks like we're going to be here for a while,
my name is Martin"
"it's been a pleasure speaking with you Martin,
you can call me Abe"

— *John Schumacher*

angus young in the autry house

tradition supersedes religion
a ceremonial rite more hallowed than breed's virility,
folklore passed down from generation to generation
no invitation required;
carpe diem performs at every gala

the backyard southern fish fry:

seductive fall temperatures
the furious bon fire, master of ceremony,
reigns supreme
an aroma once indoctrinated, never leaves the skin
life is nonexistent outside the circular glow of the blaze
faces rubicund, eyes hypnotized by flame
a single flood light desecrates
only to be outdone by the music thrashing the neighborhood

"she was a fast machine she kept her motor clean,
she was the best damn woman that i ever seen"

canned beer, the lone beverage,
cascades rapidly down gullets
primal instincts materialize like ghosts from the fire
communication slides back in time to
a language of a bygone era,
consonants dropped, vowels extended
guttural linguistics draws everyone closer

a single memory retold slaughters the floodgates,
stories gush forth, decimating the dam of decorum
the conversation decibel rises to keep pace
"you burn a cinder block pit fire out here?!"

"what did you use for the batter, just flour?!"
"no, House Autry with a little cayenne pepper!"

"she had the sightless eyes telling me no lies,
knocking me out with those American thighs"

350 degree peanut oil - a virgin canvas,
begging for the initial brushstroke
the sacrificial flounder penetrates the unctuous liquid;
sizzles, crackles,
then submissively descends
she begins her transformation
then slowly floats back to the surface,
a caramelized Phoenix

a belligerent Confederate flag,
snaps in the breeze
stalwart oak trees, once used for
lynching two centuries ago,
mutely serve as the fete's protective honor guard

— *John Schumacher*

night's chorus

the sun is gone
only whispers of the day remain
distant engines roar to find a destination
random voices echo the successes, failures of the day
a lone dog barks at nothing, neighborhood canines respond in full
symphony
crickets sing, yearning for another of its species
a gentle breeze forces oak limbs to stretch
dead leaves fall to the soft earth,
their final resting place
miles above a raindrop falls,
aching to be heard,
triumphs atop a tin roof

— *John Schumacher*

I Do Not Remember My Roots

No, no, I don't want one, you pleaded. As if you had a choice. Are you sure? Your hair will be so long, she insisted. You heard beautiful, and were confused. You were not sure, you were adamant. The stupidity of her question left you dumbfounded. Don't put your hand on active stove eyes, don't look directly at the sun, don't set fire to your hair.

didn't your mom get you a perm
child, you got some thick hair
your hair is too nappy
didn't your mom get
child, you got
your hair
didn't
child

Mommy, I want a relaxer, you said. You did want one, your desire was genuine. You listened to their lies and deceived yourself. Later, you would learn, you just wanted the words to stop. Beauty hurts, but assimilation sears. As your hair ignited, the words burned too. The beautician's chair was the kind of plastic that screeched with every minute movement you made. Your hairdresser spewed garbage and contributed to the salon's cacophony of untruths. By the time you reached seventh grade, you thought your hair had stopped growing. You didn't realize it was your psyche that was stunted. Stunted, but alive. Living paycheck to paycheck was surviving. Your mother wanted you to thrive. Language was another crucial role in your assimilation. Your mother taught you ebonics then banned the language. This language could not be spoken at home, and soon you forgot how to speak it. A mirror reflected your chalky image. Your mother beamed. A perfect fit.

Your mother taught you life emerges from flames. Each day was scalding. You set your identity ablaze and poured it into a porcelain mold. The remaining hours were spent asleep. Racism and discrimination were like the murmur of a television show on low volume. The Star Spangled Banner was deafening. Racists were rednecks in rural towns. The Confederate flag was in textbooks, not your middle class suburbia. When prejudice came from a black person, your porcelain shattered.

At lunch, when your friend asked you what classes you'd be taking the next semester, you replied with honors this, and honors that. The cafeteria: where belly laughs and smacking mouths masked the segregation. A stranger with a stranger posse strode past the whites only sign, and stopped at your table. She blurted you taking those white people classes? You're like an oreo, black on the outside, white on the inside. Each smug syllable was accompanied by a swish of her waist length braids. You heard an insult, and were confused. You heard high academic performance wasn't in the definition of authentic blackness, you heard your experience wasn't valid, you heard you couldn't exist without sacrificing your skin. Well, ain't you got something to say, she spat.

A millenia elapsed, and, still, you didn't have a response. She extinguished your internal hellfire in that small eternity. The bell rang. The moment whizzed by. You tried to relight your fire but were left with embers. You attempted to pour yourself back into porcelain. You remembered the mold was beyond repair. You couldn't recall what else occurred at school that day. At home you rushed to the bathroom mirror. You rubbed off the chalky exterior. You severed all your scorched strands. You marveled in your reflection. You stopped wishing you were white. You wish you could've told the girl with the long braids, "This is what a black girl looks like."

— *Kaylin Moss*

The Year I Fell Asleep

Home is a southern pecan tree under the summer's glaze.
It is baked with a red velvet that your grandmother's mother's
maid made.
It is frosted with a cream cheese icing thicker than the hair in
your friend's high top fade.

When your college sent you home you reveled in your extend-
ed spring break.
New Yorkers took their corporate conference calls from your
beach.
Locals rollerbladed in your downtown's cobblestoned streets.
You sought space in squares of green.

Squares of green held outdoor classes for your
Zoom University. Squares of green held hands that held
hands with yours. Squares of green green grass green lights
green leafs on palm trees beckoning you to the beach
OH the life you lived on small designated squares of green;
PARK CLOSED. CITY OF CHARLESTON.

You never knew a home that could close a beach.
You always knew a home that could kill me.

Some, say you woke up.
I, fell asleep.

I had been dozing off for a while.
Somewhere after Trayvon Martin.

Why did I attend a protest in 2016?
Tell me why.

Which black person died?
I am exhausted.

A soul food restaurant is hemorrhaging,
and in the same neighborhood,
you sleep in your million dollar home.

Why shouldn't I catch up on my sleep?

— *Kaylin Moss*

We are, America

I am, America.
My beauty glows.
I welcome the night, it illuminates my dark radiance.

Owls,
Convince them of my intelligence.
You bred me for servitude, my servitude bred wisdom.

Moon,
Exhibit my strength.
Pull the tides with the force of my power.
I learned how to endure hell, and taught my children.

Stars,
Show them how I shine.
My skin absorbs the sun.
This coily hair, is full, stunning.
Look, at my wide eyes, twinkling.

I know you see me, because you are a broken mirror.
You attempt to mimic my beauty.
Injecting lips, darkening skin, widening hips.
Cracks, in the mirror. Puddles, in the reflection.

We are, America.
You, are not us.

— *Kaylin Moss*

Body Language

When you were nothing but words on a screen,

                              your words frightened me.
Your words told me that you did not want to meet until,

                         you lost more weight.

My words should have opposed yours, but our love started
with the fear of you. It began with me inflating my ego with
the oxygen of people who looked like you. Days later you are
removing your shirt and I am terrified of what exists under-
neath. Weeks and you are flinching each time I touch your
stomach. Months and we are shopping to accommodate your
extra large, extra wide, extra long everything but why are you
extra? People who do not look like you are the baseline in a
broken system. Today I am kissing your stomach. I still look
for you in the upper right margin of the dictionary. Maybe
now I will find you.

Fatphobia:

                         the fear of you.
— *Kaylin Moss*

Growing from Diseased Soil

We believe
medicines
will expel
diseases from the
physical objects
that anchor us
to this Earth.

What happens
when a virus
infects my mind?

How many
cc's of therapy
until I'm cured?

It took me 21 seasons to learn that my mind doesn't contain a
virus to be extinguished.
Someone thought her anxiety was exterminated.
Someone thought her anxiety crawled out of the darkness and
consumed her.
Someone thought she was a pecan tree in bloom until anxiety
shriveled her roots.

Someone molded hallways into runways and dreams into
OnlyBlackFemaleInTheRoom realities.
What happens if whoever thought those shrunken thoughts
resurfaces inside my mind?
I don't use drugs because I fear losing self control, anxiety is
the fear of the unknown.

That person who thought those shrunken thoughts resurfaced last week. 11pm at night. I remembered my tools, breathed deeply twice, listened to music, and debunked worst case imaginary plot lines. It didn't work. I lost my air. The lack of oxygen created a pulsing pain behind my right eye. I called for help. I survived.

— *Kaylin Moss*

Put your boys to bed with dirty feet

They're only small and
after all the ratio
of clean-bed to growing-body
is statistically in your favor.
So his bed is still clean
Even if he brings into his dreams
The pirate battles, bug safaris,
And kickball victories of the day past
Still between his tiny clenched toes.

Put your boys to bed with dirty feet

So when they put themselves to sleep
In a home of their own
Making they will know that it's okay
To do only the best that you can
When you can, and that the inevitable
End to each day doesn't always need
To be a banishing, a washing
Down the drain.

Sometimes you take it with you,
And change the sheets in the morning.

— *Latanya Mueller*

If you've ever cut down a very old tree

You've born witness to the
perfect
Balance of life's goals and accomplishment potential.

Goals:
 Acquire: water
Sun
Soil
Produce: Height, Strength
Fight: the wind, rain, pests, people who hunt
Your ever-reaching arms.
Recognize: the strength of many (leaves).
Mourn: the loss of what sustains you (leaves).
Be nourished: from the things you have let go (leaves).
Let the little pieces of you be piled into vast,
Comforting piles, for future generations
To play in.

Accomplishments:
Shaded: the weary and hot.
Housed: the winged and crawling (many varieties).
Decorated: with ever changing color (in youth)
and eyelashes of lichen, locks of moss,
the trappings of beauty made new (in anciency).
Fed: termites, campfires, the ire of men with chainsaws and
        too much free time.
Balanced: on deep hollowed roots, on wood piles.

Shined: as firelight dancing in the expectant eyes
of small children, holding your sticks to cook
the most perfect
caramel marshmallow.

— *Latanya Mueller*

I find it hard to say

 That your lips riffs
Fall like music in the air.
A tumbling, rolling casacara of
"You should say..."
        "Don't you know..."
                "Why can't you just..."
                        "All I wanted was..."

Yet somehow on a fogged road
The headlights of two cars pass
A collision narrowly avoided.
The drivers visibly shaken.

                        Almost.

— *Latanya Mueller*

Tiny, perfect things.

Every hundred mornings I find
That the bubbles in my coffee form
A perfect clover.
It is markable, but unremarkable in that
I am not Irish so I have to content myself
With the harmony of things coming in threes.
There is no magic there for me.

Tiny, perfect things.

I walk through my day with the spectre
Of your heartbeat in the palm of my hand
From the last time I pressed it to your chest
My face nuzzled in your neck
My untamable main of curls tangled between your fingers
Deep breaths: together. Time: frozen. Sleep: creeping in.

Tiny, perfect things.

— *Latanya Mueller*

A Love Letter to My Students

Students,
Brief years yield big choices.
In these four school walls
I am blessed to fertilize thoughts
And water voices
Into tall tall trees who stand
On their own.

I am not perfect.
The sea of my mind swims with
Ideas and good intention
With plots and plans too vast to mention.
And I promise the reason I
Demand excellence is because if
I do not, you might always hide
What's inside: genius.

Life's not perfect.
Life can be bold and bloody
Or doubtful and defiant, leaving you
Skeptical, scared, skating by.
That, too, was I
When I was young.

We have been put together by
Laws we haven't read by
Dead people long in their graves why
Should we go to ours adversaries

And not accomplices?
As confederates.
Comrades.
An Intelligence Allegiance.

Sometimes I cry because I
Wonder if you are crying
Out there
Somewhere.

I care.

— *Latanya Mueller*

Christmas Eve in the Garden

Christmas eve,
alone in my garden,
standing still in moist blades of grass,
watching the dogs
mingle in moonlight,

I close my eyes remembering...

Frost clutched every windowpane,

Pajama-clad children bundled in snowsuits,

Nonna's linguine drenched in homemade marinara,

Aunt Mary's date drops covered in coconut,

Tito's vodka in a stem glass with ice and lemons,

Split-level house packed with people and presents,

*Laughter bouncing into the front yard garden covered in
snow...*

Christmas eve's moon emerges,
solitary in the vast sky,
illuminating the garden,
my wistful tears watering
bulbs of new flowers yet to bloom,
planted under dogs' paws.

— *Linda Joy Walder*

Return to Flight

The plane rises
as champagne bubbles
elevate my courage
after two years grounded.

Ascending above celestial clouds
I do not find you,
though I feel you traveling with me
while the champagne helps me glide
through thick air.

At the gate,
assisted by the lingering effervescence
of champagne bubbles,
I claim the baggage bearing my name,
carrying it onward, as I go.

— *Linda Joy Walder*

Cubism

Hummingbird soul
silver leaf
crystal Lalique
Hebi snake
still life
lemon light
salmon flowers
mermaid priestess
Staffordshire zebra figurines
flicker of hope in pink

— *Linda Joy Walder*

Rainbow Light (for Evelyn)

Your light sparkles
like a thousand fireworks
shot briskly into the sky.

Oh how the plain folk admire you,
and the loudmouthed fear you,
passionless souls hanging on to a thread of Joseph's coat.

But you,
you create your days
from pioneer sweat and stone walls glistening,
then reinvent yourself
in moonlit scenes.

Yes, you are bright,
Yes, you shine,
on, and on and on.

Even if the colors of the rainbow fade,
you never will.

— *Linda Joy Walder*

Cosmic Connection

I feel your eyes
Soft,
Glowing upon me
As I see a fire
Deep
Within the depths
Of your soul.
I try to hold you,
But you sift
Through my hands
Like grains of sand.
As the grandfather clock ticks,
And the new becomes old,
We float
Through time and space.
We fade
Into one.
We last
Forever.

— *Lucinda Rowekamp*

Antique Shop

Put me on your shelf or
Put me in your china cabinet
So I can be nothing
But admired.
Let me collect the dust
That falls through the air.
Leave me be,
Just look at me
Through the glass.
Let me become timeless.
Let me be one of many
In your special antique shop.

— *Lucinda Rowekamp*

The Hardest Love

Loving yourself comes from
A scary place.
It is unknown territory
A place that has been clouded
By stormy people
And bad decisions.
Loving yourself comes from
A state of desperation.
Once the smoke clears
And the clouds lift
The sun will shine
A golden beam upon you,
And you will look at yourself
And hear yourself scream
"There you are! I've been waiting for you!"
And fall into your own arms,
Cry from the warm embrace,
And thank yourself that you decided
To come home at last.

— *Lucinda Rowekamp*

Equal Affection

I walk through the streets of New York City
My heels, clicking on the pavement
My breath, clouded in the brisk air.
The snowflakes, falling upon my cheeks
And your hand, curled around mine.
I look at the skyscrapers and think,
If equal affection cannot be displayed,
Then how will the young ever learn to love?
This is why I hold your hand tightly
And bring it close to my lips
And kiss it gently, just like you would do to me.
Isn't that what equality is?
If equal affection cannot be measured,
Then neither can time.
There are endless limits for both,
And my love for you is infinite.

— *Lucinda Rowekamp*

The Art of Being Human

People are greedy, all they want is more.
Humbleness is easy to ignore, but jealousy is not.
Emptiness stirs in the belly and is later transformed.
They walk through life like everything is a bore.
Wasting time while on autopilot,
People are greedy, all they want is more.
Complain about something every day,
learning to conform
To office jobs and city life, lost hopes and dreams
These feelings only build, they can't be transformed.
If civilians could look within themselves
They would realize
everything they crave is already there.
People are greedy, all they want is more.
The loss of themselves is the only thing they mourn
To trust God and to look their demons in the face,
Only then will these negative feelings be transformed.
It's okay to lose a sense of self,
As long as one is conscientious and aware,
People are greedy, all they want is more.
The art of being human, is greed can be transformed.

— *Lucinda Rowekamp*

Confidence flows through the sleeves of this blue stripped flannel. Soft and conformed, it embraces my arms and lays perfectly on my collar bone. It tagged along on coffee dates, literature classes and writing sessions. The colors always complimenting my complexion. "I really like that flannel," he says smiling. My cheeks flush rose and the only thought I can muster to speak is, "thanks, me too."

— The Blue Stripped Flannel

— Maci Petrolle

and I ran
the leaves crunched loudly under my feet
I needed to stop for air but
my feet kept moving
my lungs kept breathing
and no one told me when to stop
I could feel my face burning up
the ache beginning in my ankles
I was always told there was an end point
but I do not see one in the distance
I just see pavement
a small river
abandon homes
and the sound of persistent footsteps
inching closer
and closer
trying to keep up

— anxiety is a beast

— Maci Petrolle

cherry stained lips,
wine glass,
some guys are genuinely good.
some are too good to be true.

betrayal of the heart,
the mind,
the bones,
how can one who claims to love me,
lie while starting directly into my brown hues?

one glass down,
three more to go,
filing the painful void,
clinging to the feeling of numbness,
i find myself slowly letting you go.

— leaving you in the past

— Maci Petrolle

Forgotten Drummer

Oh, the forgotten
Drummer who keeps the hard beat.
He keeps playing in hopes I will
Eventually follow His rhythm.
I hear His stomps and brushes
At midnight when I am most awake.
I hear His wild call in the setting hours
As I settle into slumber time.
My own drummer boy, my God, my shepherd
Who is in the background with His
Sticks and pedals pounding away begging
Me to sing out and cry His name.
I hear you.
I love you.
I will cry out and sing your name.

— *Marilyn Cox*

Flower Meditation

Get comfortable.
Close your eyes and breathe through your nose and
exhale through your mouth.
Again.
Again.
Keep closing your eyes.
Now, open them.
What do you see?
A rose.
Look closely at the rose.
Each petal caresses each other like how the human fam-
ily works.
Look at the color of each petal, the shape of the leaf, and
each nodule in the stem.
Its beauty is overwhelming.
Now, return to your body.
What is that thought?
You are like the flower.
Your skin is your soul's envelope.
It has a unique stamp.
You were delivered to earth for a reason.
Open your envelope and see what is inside.
I find your beauty overwhelming.

— *Marilyn Cox*

Color

I need color to stay alive. I am not afraid to say it.
Take star sapphire. I see compassion.
Take onyx. I see suffering.
Take coral. I see masochism of the earthly heart.
I can't live anymore without the colors from strangers
that bleed.
Pop, pop, pop.
That is what color sounds like.
The jewel tones have music if you are quiet.
Me, I need color to wake me up.
Colors glow in the night.
Colors take risks.
Colors pop.

— *Marilyn Cox*

Avocado

My life is like an attempt to carve an avocado.
Making beauty marks around a dark pit in my stomach.
I know one day the soft green flesh will rot and die,
But I vow to keep carving
so one day I can take a picture and
Make a heart memory of the beauty that once was.

— *Marilyn Cox*

Tree Poem

The wind woke me up
when my poem blew into a magnolia tree.
It was springtime, when every good person dies.
While the hydrangeas bloomed,
she died again and I remembered
Her rant on cookie cutters and tying everything into a
nice neat bow.
The scourge of the cookie cutter makes me laugh now
that I have her set.
I am not making any two cookies alike.
The poem in the tree hasn't been read aloud.
It seems I will need a help from a friendly giant.
All the other people
are just not tall enough to reach it yet.

— *Marilyn Cox*

Haiku #1

My altar is like
a porch light I leave on in
case someone visits.

— Natasha Akery

Haiku #2

Cypress knees: totems
accepting offerings of
pine needles and leaves.

— Natasha Akery

Haiku #3

A man and his bike
stranded on a median,
cars swarming like sharks.

— *Natasha Akery*

The Last Rose of Summer

On a beautiful summer day, a rose
pose, as its flower, catch my eye.
Tranquility and beauty and passion,
and harmony manifest a festive
of order, for the last rose of summer.

In a circle of a year,
echo a battle of winter,
spring, summer and fall.
A phase, so softly blowing
echo, an epic battle.

A ballet, of flower dancing
and the leaves falling to
a poetic ballad of
poem, a sonnet,
of color to capture visions.

My eye's on the last day of summer
for the last rose of summer
as a sculptor sculpts the stone
with his day the craft is
the last rose of summer.

In nature, poetic art, and
artist, a grand prize.
every flower has its
own beauty to delight.

and enlighten the beauty
and grace, and artist,
paint a picture in time
one day at a time,
to sculpt and craft.

It's lost, thus simplicity,
splendor, now the summer
has gone, and the winter
has come, she smiles
in her eyes.

The posey posing a picture,
unmeasure a believing
treasure in the
last rose of summer.

— *Randy Milledge*

The Fox In The Field

Oh my lord, sometimes I feel
just like the fox in the field.

Oh man oh man, the hand that rocks the cradle,
women and man. oh my lord sometimes
I feel like the whole world
closing in on me, man.

Oh my some times I feel
like a fox, just like the fox in the field, people
say wait but weight broke the wagon.

They say take the cotton out of your ears
and put it in your mouth. Close your mouth
and listen and learn.
A closed mouth don't get fed
and nothing brings the fish
out of the water but it's mouth.

Oh lord sometimes I feel
just like the fox in the field.
I been running both day and night,
sometimes I feel so tired.

Now even a poor rat got more
than one hole to claw in.
The birds of the sky nest in the tree.
Even the fish of the sea
have the valley and stream.

Every land has a castle, every
castle has a hound dog,
and every hound dog
has a master, and every
man has a soul.

Never grow old nor weary
for the labor they say
is hard, but it's fair.
Need no ticket and it costs
nothing for the spirit.

So start dancing and prancing
to the power of faith. Hold
up your hand rejoice in jubilee.
Hallelujah is the highest praise.

Oh man, sometimes I feel just
like the fox in the field.

— *Randy Milledge*

I Don't Mind the Years

standing in a down
pour with my eyes closed
I can see a dry place beneath
my skin resting unknowable

stepping out into a fresh
blue coat of paint each
day clears the clovers
from my ears completely

there's no key solving
the doors of our opening
into pastures of cats
drawing their dreams

letting the haiku go
free to seek a telescope
to watch an idea
fence a line between us

canyons wrecked and rusty
lying in place of a real
loss of fear invented
to wear daily blinding

space debris floating across
the black inside my mirror
tells me nothing I can hold
will keep my heart beating

instead of running my feet
connect me to the ground
forever and I have no
choice in the matter

there's a tall long shadow
loosening its grip
on my ankles and candles
are in my eyes

I don't mind the years
going by the window
it's too much to talk
about love in France

no one can look
me in the eye too deeply
for a silent fish
is my hopeful friend

I know only a few
things for sure
I'm doing the same nothing
every time perfectly

— *Roger Mindwater*

Almost a Day

I'm placing clothes on an invisible
mannequin leaning in the window

if the sun rang the doorbell today
I would be unprepared in the corner

I'm searching for a photograph
of the way you don't see me

there's circles all over the globe
that lead my fingers farther away

down the river kids are building
boats for the coming winter

the grass and leaves turn according
to ancient bird flight patterns

the shadows cut wrinkles in
our faces every year ever sweeter

I'm just getting in the groove of
a record lying in the mud

I'm doing cartwheels in the closet
while the backyards laugh loud

find me impossible in an armchair
sitting and calling it accidental

a warm blinding blanket over
the coughing leftover farewells

I'm mining beneath the floorboard
flowers for a bed to rest in

I hear the train from my house
but I don't run to meet my sister

sometimes a day is just out of reach

— *Roger Mindwater*

No Shoes?

the sky is leaking glass again
I'm sitting under the spotlight
pictures painted all around

you went to the mountains
sitting on a map of my fingerprints
with an empty glass of water

crying in the frozen food isle
is one of my favorite pastimes
of unmeasurable proportions

keep my thoughts instead of lying
in the grass beside my wonder
at the unbelievable clouds

I can't help anyone find their shoes
so I can't hold myself in the night
just listening to the up and down

— *Roger Mindwater*

Hello, Can You Hear Me?

this is a telegram to the troubadour of dirt
mountain
   I have a small thin line fishing
for the chance to meet some scarlet
cloudburst
    most of my meaning disappears
around the canyon corner into no one
looking at any time of day
       I am a furious wish
for skin I have never felt

how can I hope to assemble the rivers
of the world into a language fit for human
headspace
    what is the frequency connecting
the courage of certain soundscapes
        I can't find
the shapes you hold me with a sunset every
hour of the day dreaming

I'm trying every possible potential
bend in the road
    rushing rambling
to paint a babbling underground
worthy of your slow hand smoothing

no telling which combination is the key
to the universe
    in two halves together

— *Roger Mindwater*

Vulnerability

On the rare occasion, I bite my lips.
I bite my lips when I'm mad.
I don't say mad because I hardly ever picture myself as
an animal, except when I'm mad.
On the rare occasion I bite my lips
when I feel I'm about to slip.
Slip into a reality that will swallow my soul whole.
I bit my lips less than three months ago.
I've been kneading at the bottom lip for more than two
years now.
I'm harassed by my thoughts, my memories,
my condition, my longing,
my desire to control happiness,
and my lapse in judgement that leads me to a place
where I forget to embrace joy.
Vulnerable, open, exposed, at the mercy of others...all
words that terrify those resistant to the challenges life
brings.

I bite my lips occasionally. Sometimes when unexpected
joy enters the room. I become vulnerable, exposed, visible to those whose thoughts may betray my joy.

I bite my lips when I'm angry.

 Upset with myself because... because I let you get close
enough to break my heart, upset with myself
because I let you disappoint me, upset with myself
because I continue to disappoint me, upset with myself
because I continue to underestimate me, upset with
myself because I continue to care that you
underestimate me.

I bite my lips when I know my too much is just the
beginning. I have that moment when I hesitate, afraid to
relinquish a control that I never had.
Afraid that vulnerability will overwhelm and the mask
will shatter into pieces so miniscule
they'd defy definition.

I bite my lips trying to preserve the myth
that my vulnerability will destroy me.

I knead and I nibble on my bottom lip hoping the words
won't penetrate, praying the grief won't breakthrough,
and narrowly trusting that the temple won't crumble.

I bit my lips until the bites, the stifling,
the push downwards, and resentment of joy hurt more
than the grief and the vulnerability combined.

I used to bite my lips!

— *Samajema Davis*

Remaining Confident

I am no longer bowing down to your indifference.
I am not swayed by your confident lie.
I am no longer a slave to try.
I will forever now be guided by the Trinity reference.

Remaining Confident

I smile and wish you well.
I refuse to be influenced by your perpetual state of
ignorance led petty
I embrace growth but now I see, you you are not ready
You'd rather be right than ready; that I can tell.

Remaining Confident

My love is righteous and loyal
My love language is sincerity
I will now only participate in things that contribute to
my prosperity
I will no longer walk in common; I am royal.

Remaining Confident

The Trinity reference designed me prosperous
In Spirit, I grow
Through struggle I know
I stand in this truth; not to be boisterous

I chose to Remain Confident

I have found forgiveness to be a friend
I release guilt from your never trying
Everyone's fault for your coldness I'm not buying

Not giving up on you but the length of my branch has come to an end

Remaining Confident

I am a child of the Most High.
My intent is to focus on the light
And when darkness comes, I'm assured it won't always be night.
I'm thriving, I'm not just getting by.

I choose to Remain Confident

— *Samajema Davis*

Too Many Attachments

You've got many attachments to ever love me.
You're attached to highs that you'll never feel again
Attached to hearts that you'll never help mend.
Attached to a body you'll never give your best.
Never attached to who you want to be.

You're attached to praise that isn't really praise.
Attached to entertaining those who never intend for your
soul to rest.
Attached to demons that won't let go.
Attached to evading love and embracing lust.
Never attached to the kind of self-love that will amaze.

You're attached to a surface kind of you.
Attached to you in a box.
Attached to a shadow that drags you back in.
Attached to an easy that never sees you grow
Never attached to the Spirit that surely sees us through.

You're attached to unexplored pain.
Attached to generational curses.
Attached to being afraid to want more.
Attached to swallowing anguish and truth.
Never attached to growth and lasting gain.

You're attached to never hitting the bottom.
Attached to lies.
Attached to infliction.
Attached to wanting more than what you can give.
Never attached to, "no girl that's not him."

You've got too many attachments to be attached.

— *Samajema Davis*

Needles and Mountains

I realize that God loves him. I am resolved to not
mention his name but I'll say the name of his victim.
I say George Floyd, I say George is Abel and he, the
killer, is Caine.
He asked the question, Am I my brother's keeper and
said no.... because he's a rusty corroded gear in the
system.

What happens when the system oppresses reason and
compassion?
What happens when it believes it cannot function
without suppression?
What happens when it feeds into greed and insecurity
mixed; capitalism
What happens when someone has to be on top?
What happens when the top is a needle point and the
foundation a crumbling mountain, heavy from the
weight of a needle point's fascism
The narrow, the small minded, the peace hating, and
order loving fight to control the story
So the oppressed suppress until their voices cry out in
blazes of glory
We are not going to be quiet, we are not going to stay
dormant, we won't only puff smoke and the occasional
ash...we breathe out deep bemoaning breaths and exhale
fire.
Flaming fire, flickering flames alternating between blue
and white hot.
We express anger, regret, pain, frustration, but most
importantly hope.
It's the language of the oppressed and it draws their ire.
It's the language of an Abel, someone who toils day and

night and produces greatness, only to have their spoils plundered and belittled because God likes it best.
The needle sticking out from the mountain thinks it deserves it all because it has the better view.
But that's the thing, it doesn't. It has the whole landscape at its disposal but it never sees the whole sky.

It's too focused on its own reflection and it's blinding in the sun and in the light of the moon.
The foundation arranged it so it could see on a swivel but it cemented itself in one direction... unable to move...and as the mountain continues to move it starts to crumble from the resistance.
The mountain crumbles from violent resistance to views of the entire landscape.
But the needle point fails to realize that a crumbled mountain is still a mountain, with all its bits and pieces it's still mighty and strong.

It bubbles and brims with hope, expectation, and long overdue demands for reparations.
And now the pieces are like dry bones rising from the dead becoming the ONE they were meant to be all along.
So what about the needle with all its gears? It's still struggling to stay atop.
Still rigid and still poisoning it's gears with fear, half-truths, and conditional love.
Still refusing to budge but there's hope
because the foundation designed it see on a swivel and the gears...well God loves them,
They just don't understand yet.

When they do, everything they do, they'll regret.

— *Samajema Davis*

Swallowing Disappointment

I find myself getting used to swallowing disappointment
and it's disappointing me.
I discern and I ignore discernment.
I know you but I continue to give the benefit of the
doubt... all the while knowing and
swallowing disappointment.
I bend and I bend but I don't break becoming more like
rubber than love.
Wrapping myself in your words and ignoring your deeds.
But the rubber is stretching beyond it's ability and will
most certainly pop
I find myself swallowing disappointment and right now
it's stuck...heavy...and laying on my heart.

— *Samajema Davis*

North of Seventy

Well, I have finally reached the town called
North of Seventy.
It is beautiful here!
The pace is slower, and the lights are dimmed lower.
No one is in a rush in the town of
North of Seventy.
You can amble and wander at your very own pace—
No hurrying, no scurrying, no trying to make haste.

In North of Seventy,
We not only stop to smell the roses,
But we also will stop to drink the coffee, or tea,
Or perhaps sip a little wine or brandy.
We are not too judgmental in
North of Seventy.

In North of Seventy
Our music is slow and sweet.
And though our hearing is not quite as sharp,
We are most likely to hear with our heart.
So, we can dance to the rhythm of what we feel,
Not to the clang, twang, bang, or loud peal!

Of course, in North of Seventy
Our sight is not what it used to be,
But somehow, we see the world more clearly.
One might say we have less sight but more vision.
We are equipped with special filters
In North of Seventy:
We see what others cannot, and what others see,
Is of little consequence in the town of North of Seventy.

In North of Seventy
We love deeply and give love freely.
I guess we have come to realize that
If you have arrived whole
To the town of North of Seventy,
It is because of TRUE LOVE,
The one that can only come from ABOVE!

So today, I meditate and celebrate
My arrival to North of Seventy!
I'll take off my shoes and wiggle my toes,
Maybe shovel and rake
And chop pesky weeds with my hoe.
I'll eat what I want, maybe something a little sweet,
We tend to savor the small moments in North of Seventy.
Because we know this is not our final destination
We have so much more to do and so much more to see,
In places far beyond North of Seventy!

— *Shelia L. Anderson*

My ROGI

I have a FROG in my house!
I call my FROG "ROGI."
Oh, it's not the green, bug-eyed,
Fast-tongued kind of frog.
No, it's a room over my garage—
A Finished-Room-Over-Garage.
Except I call mine, "ROGI":
"Room-of-Good-Intentions."

In my ROGI are generations of photos,
In boxes, in bags, peeping
From crooks and crannies
Longing to have a home
In the hundred bucks worth of empty albums
I intended to secure them in.
These dear mementos deserve such a place!
At least, that was my desire and intention.

A gang of ghosts of Christmases, long past
Haunts my ROGI.
Plastic tombs just can't hold them down!
They slip and slither from their holes
Of red, green, silver, and gold;
Only to be crushed to smithereens
Upon unscheduled visits up the stairs.
My intentions were to color-code the boxes
Of bells and baubles;
Toss out darkened, lifeless lights;
Rewind red ribbons on cardboard spindles,
For I intend to use them again and again.
So, they can stay in the ROGI.

Oh, how can I forget the books I will read?
And the weathered and warn ones, that I have?
Why, I intend to pass them on to some
Deserving erudite, such as myself, of course!
The relics of my profession
Certainly, are useful in some novice's class.
I will give them away,
Without anyone ever having to ask.
Those are my intentions, anyway,
When I find time to sort them out:
The "keeps" and the "goes."

And I still have a desk in my ROGI,
My sewing machine, and some perfectly
Good dress-making patterns—
Not a cut on them! Vintage!
Why, with the way prices are sky-rocketing
On clothes made in China,
I may as well go back to making my own!
I just need to go through my notions basket,
And gather up my sewing tools, and
Viola! I'm back in business!
I definitely intend to return to sewing.

And while I'm up here,
I may as well use this big exercise ball.
After all these years,
The thing has not deflated!
(But I have certainly inflated!)
I can drop these few pounds and inches
I've been meaning to work off around the middle.
Who needs a gym?
I can work out right here in my ROGI—
As soon as I find the instructions
That came with the ball.

And I have absolutely no intention
Of letting these dead bugs stay up here any longer!
How in the world did these critters get in here?
This is a ROGI after all-
Not a "frog!"
Heaven forbids that something slithers
Or crawls up here for a quick meal!
No, cleaning my ROGI is way at the top of my to-do list,
At least, I think it was.
It must be lost among my other projects.
I'll never accomplish anything without my list.
I've got to do better.
I intend to do better.
My ROGI will become a FROG one day,
Just as it was intended to be!

— *Shelia L. Anderson*

Memorial Day

Memorial Day suddenly has new meaning for me:
I have a serviceman: my baby boy.
Memorial Day: a day to remember
The lost in battle and the living lost.
Seem merely boys and girls.
Some left parts of their body and soul
In a foreign place, never to retrieve.
It's hard for those who went for work
And not a noble cause. Harder still
For those who can't discern the cause,
Except now, their own survival.
Who sends our sons and daughters off to war?
Who orders the time and place?
They are safely at home:
Parading up and down the streets,
With flags waving, horns blaring, drums beating--
Or, perhaps, just sleeping in late.
Remember those who served and simply survived—
And especially those who did not, on Memorial Day.

— *Shelia L. Anderson*

Paradox

There is a paradox I see--
One that has always perplexed me:
That my brothers of lighter hue
Can look down on us who are darker,
As if not fully human, too.
So, explain to me, my light-skinned brothers,
The blond hair,
Butter-colored skin,
And eyes of blue,
Born among us of darker hue?

— *Shelia L. Anderson*

Church with Granny

I went to church with Granny today
And it was kind of strange, I'll say.
People were dancin', laughin' and cryin'.
So, I started laughin' and dancin', too.
But it wasn't till Granny took me outside,
Saying, "I'm not through with you!"
Next thing you know, I'm cryin', too!

— *Shelia L. Anderson*

The Poem in Which I Finally Say Their Names (An Unending Verse)

~~It is with sorrow, no wait.~~ **Sandra Bland** ~~Start over.~~ **Rayshard Brooks** ~~I am here today to.~~ **Eleanor Bumpurs** ~~*shakes head*~~ **Michael Brown** ~~Wrong.~~ **Michelle Cusseaux** ~~The skeleton of a poet sits wearily by a boiling river.~~ **Philando Castile** ~~She watches words flow instead of blood.~~ **Deborah Danner** ~~He etches the stone tablets on his knees.~~ **Jordan Davis** ~~No more tears.~~ **Janisha Fonville** ~~Yes, more.~~   **George Floyd** ~~There are more tears than I can cry.~~ **Darnesha Harris** ~~Fresh death weekly.~~ **Eric Garner** ~~And the echoes grow louder. For concrete pillows.~~ **Kathryn Johnston** ~~For Skittles and ice tea and cell phones in pockets.~~ **Trayvon Martin** ~~So what if my music is loud? For feeding hungry people.~~ **Cynthia Graham Hurd, Rev. DePayne Middleton-Doctor, Rev. Dr. Daniel Simmons, Sr., Ethel Lee Lance, Rev. Sharonda Ann Coleman-Singleton, Susie J. Jackson, Tywanza Sanders, Myra Thompson, Rev. Clementa C. Pinckney** ~~My wallet is in my pocket. Do not take me into custody. I am already in custody.~~ **Aiyana Jones** ~~The created glitch is in the system.~~ **David McAtee** ~~I am not who you think I am. Am not.~~   **Charleena Lyles** ~~I have been on the ground for four hours. Me? Twelve.~~ **Dreasjon Reed** ~~Minding my own business is not enough. Jogging in the morning is not enough. Breathing is too much.~~ **Gynnya McMillen** ~~Wish I could jump overboard into a sea of forgetfulness and still be alive.~~ **Tamir Rice** ~~I was playing with a toy gun. But I'm just trying to go to work. Blown out like a candle. I was sleeping in my own bed.~~ **Breonna Taylor** ~~Sleeping with my grandmother on our couch. I was selling loose cigarettes.~~ **James Scurlock** ~~Have a bachelor party. Get a cup of joe.~~ **Alesia Thomas** ~~What was his name again?~~ **Walter Scott** ~~I must remember her. Can't forget him. Don't forget.   Remember. Remember. Remember. Please forgive me for not knowing all of your names!~~ How. Can. I. Ever. Fly. Again?

— *Yvette R. Murray*

The Case of Accomplice Liability in 43 American States (Stave v)

One hand can lift up life
as well as take.
All that is needed is.
One to be as true as
blue cannot be
if all is all
that they
see.

One hand can take a life
is the asphalt rhyme.
All that is needed is.
One to exist blackly
in a metropolis,
down home down,
any street, anywhere, any,
any

The hand of

Is one hand all
to save a life. a heart. beat.
All that is needed is.
Five fingers. Oh. Five?
A just hin, honest scales,
bring some light,
hand him some hot tea,
drink.

All one hand can
play is one song. Is.
All that is needed is.
Unbalanced forces
The. Take. Kill. Shoot.
Of thee I
Die. Right.
There.

— *Yvette R. Murray*

Come Back; Dis Ya' Home (A bop for 2020)

The problem, the elder shouted,
is louder the trees speak
the less you hear
and the less you hear
fewer recipes you remember.
Less you cook, more you eat dirt.

Come back; Dis ya' home

The problem, the elder whispered,
has been around since a white lion
since about the time that money
was money. Folk walked off plantations
into another white nightmare.
Integrations and red lines
away from rhythms, away from rhythms
that breathe underwater.

Come back; Dis ya' home

Let blood memory guide you
back to Purple mindscape!
Then you will not eat dirt.
Drink sassafrass/strong horse tea,
be a midwife or potter, sew sweetgrass
and build strong mountains again.

Come back; Dis ya' home

— *Yvette R. Murray*

Minstrel Man

They are used to being entertained by us.
Even old field hollers can move the moon
It's like something only we humans do:
A dark and dandy deed at twilight.

Even old field hollers can move the moon.
Then we paint in colors and faces.
A dark and dandy deed at twilight:
Walking in the dust of children's bones.

Then we paint in colors and faces
We got all that jig and that jive, see?
Walking in the dust of children's bones:
Could be bebop or ballet or both.

We got all that jig and that jive, see?
From Middle Passage to Carnegie Hall
Could be bebop or ballet or both:
brings satin and patent leather swan songs.

From Middle Passage to Carnegie Hall
It's like something only we humans do
bring satin and patent leather swan songs:
They are used to being entertained by us.

— *Yvette R. Murray*

Accents
After Denise Frohman

My Mama, too, has the sky in her mouth
She carries beautiful Hausa, rhythmic Igbo and exquisite
Yoruba
All smashed into one gumbo called Gullah.
Gullah: The language of survival.
In muck of rice fields
and muck of this republic
It flows with a rhythm so deep, deep, deep
It has to be eaten,
like all good gumbo should,
with cornbread.
We know that the beauty of this creole
is living on nothing
Thriving in mist
Governed by the moon itself,
Gullah
pounds the shore
like the tide
dragging grains of sand
to build islands elsewhere.
Hidden deep within our throats,
language of rebellion,
seen in the eyes,
heard in the tilt of a chin,
My Mama brought it to me
with the pride of bare feet.
Now, poachers take her like ivory
and put her on their trinkets to sell.

— *Yvette R. Murray*

You
So Damn
Skrong
And I say Skrong
With a K like
SKRONG
Cause "ST" just don't
Carry the same weight
Like k do
Like you do
You just skrong

*A Lesson in
Rhetoric*

204

You ever think
When you pluck a Rose
You kill it
Because it is beautiful
You ever think
Roses have thorns
Because they are aware
Of that beauty

An ode To Black Women
With "Attitudes"

When you're Black you're never really lonely

When a group of us get on the subway
We color _____ spaces
Our voices
       too boisterous
Africa still carries on our vocal chords
       though so far away from home
The offended face of the lady who lives on 65th and Park
       or the "inherited" coastal property
STARES
Would love to be as big
       ..but literally could neva
Curious faces are typical
For when two or more are gathered
       God is in the mist
And some people feel uncomfortable around Holy
       it aint come from quiet meditation neitha
       ain't come from no peaceful retreats
Got that Holy that come from hollers
       Come from tear drenched faces
       Knees to ground
       Broken hands pieced together
This Holy aint neva been quiet
       And aint got to be
Cause Africa Still Lingers
       Despite never having touched the soil
       Despite the lady who lives on 65th and Park
And her ugly looks
       And her grandmama ugly words
       And her grandaddies ugly rules
See we aint ugly
       We Gorgeous
       And loud as we wanna be
       Just like Holy

— *Zania Cummings*

CPSIA information can be obtained
at www.ICGtesting.com
Printed in the USA
LVHW101802030922
727556LV00005B/824

9 781737 469667